SANTA MONICA
CALIFORNIA

POSTAGE
1¼ ¢
WITHOUT
MESSAGE

Then & Now

SANTA MON

GIBBS
SMITH
Gibbs Smith, Publisher
Salt Lake City

ICA

Then & Now

Jake Klein

First Edition

07 06 05 04 03   5 4 3 2 1

Published by
Gibbs Smith, Publisher
P.O. Box 667
Layton, Utah 84041

Orders: (1-800) 748-5439
www.gibbs-smith.com

Edited by Suzanne Gibbs Taylor
Designed by Kurt Wahlner
Printed and bound in Hong Kong

Library of Congress Cataloging-in-Publication Data

Klein, Jake.
  Then & now : Santa Monica / Jake Klein.— 1st ed.
      p. cm.
  ISBN 1-58685-230-2
  1. Historic buildings—California--Santa Monica—Pictorial
works. 2. Historic sites—California—Santa Monica—Pictorial
works. 3. Architecture—California—Santa Monica--Pictorial
works. 4. Santa Monica (Calif.)—Buildings, structures, etc.—
Pictorial works. 5. Santa Monica (Calif.)—History—Pictorial
works. I. Title: Then and now. II.Title: Santa Monica. III. Title.
F869.S51 K56 2003
979.4'93--dc21
                              2003012229

Introduction

There is a powerful pioneer spirit that courses through the veins of those who are driven to tame and settle American places, and Southern California history is rife with people who were drawn to this wild land, which was utterly open and untouched by man's heavy hands. One such city is Santa Monica, an exquisite coastal jewel perched on the edge of America.

Like so many beach towns, individuals who were in dogged pursuit of escape settled Santa Monica. The rolling purple of the Santa Monica Mountains plunging headlong into the Pacific Ocean proved irresistible, even to the earliest explorers. First discovered by non-Natives in the late 1700s, this area sat undeveloped. After Spanish explorers stumbled upon this stretch of coastal mountains in 1769, wars between the United States, Mexico, and Spain separated the lands. First deeded to Mexican nationals Xavier Alvarado and Antonio Machado in 1827, Santa Monica slowly became a popular destination for campers and smugglers. The rolling hills and canyons and the unpopulated coastline were perfect havens for those pleasure (and treasure) seekers—refugees from the dusty heat of Los Angeles. By the late 1860s, Santa Monica had been discovered and a city was born.

In the increasingly industrialized world, Americans continually searched for ways to live simultaneously within and outside their own fevered urbanization. As Los Angeles's population began to spread outward from downtown, adventurous souls seeking beauty and space would migrate to surrounding communities and Santa Monica was a natural destination.

On the eve of the California land rush of the late 1800s, two men had the foresight to settle Santa Monica's wild bluffs. Senator John Percival Jones and Colonel R. S. Baker were among the first to exploit the relatively cheap acreage on these hills above the sea. The two men purchased large swaths from original landowners Alvarado, Machado, and Don Sepulveda. By 1875, the first plots of land were auctioned off to the public at the foot of what is now Wilshire Boulevard. Within nine months of the auction, the rapidly growing city had a permanent population of 1,000. By 1877, Santa Monica had a newspaper, an opera house, a church, and a school.

Santa Monica has always been a fantasy destination for travelers and a playground for the lucky people who have managed to find ways to live there.

From senators to congressmen, from movie stars to moguls and every stratum in between—the city is magnetic. Bordered on the north by Malibu and the south by Venice Beach, Santa Monica is now host to world-class beaches and is an international tourist destination. Within its boundaries, well-known architects such as Irving Gill, Richard Neutra, Charles and Ray Eames, and Frank Gehry have shaped the city. Today more than 84,000 diverse citizens call Santa Monica home.

Santa Monica was founded on a desire for pleasure and for the vibrant, creative pulse that comes with life lived on the coast. This book is a tribute to the spirit embodied by the city. From its humble roots as a dusty mining town to its status as an important part of California's future, *Then and Now: Santa Monica* is a celebration of the spirit that makes the city a destination for generations of locals and tourists alike.

—Jake Klein

▲ By the late 1800s, Santa Monica Canyon had been discovered by a burgeoning tourist class searching for new places to escape. The canyon became accessible to hundreds of people in 1875 when a railroad was built to ShooFly Landing, where Colorado Street reaches the beach today.

Known as the western Greenwich Village, Santa Monica Canyon is an artsy, rustic valley with homes priced from $500,000 to over $2 million. Modern design, as evidenced here in a flat roof and concrete building materials, has been a theme in this area since the 1930s.

▲ Sixteen years after Santa Monica was settled, the town was typically frontier, with dusty streets wide enough to turn a buggy in and lined with falsely fronted wooden buildings.

▲ Gone are the wide streets of frontier days. Cars aren't allowed on the Third Street Promenade anymore, but it's one of the most popular sites in the city and attracts an international mix of visitors. The open-air shopping district is home to unique retail shops, trendy sidewalk cafés and restaurants, nightclubs, and movie theaters.

▲ *The Evening Outlook* was Santa Monica's only newspaper when it opened in 1929. In March 1998 the *Outlook* closed its doors. Now the *Santa Monica Daily Press* building, it has remained a point of reference in the community.

▲ Across the street and in the shadow of the *Outlook* building is Santa Monica Place, two blocks from Santa Monica Pier and the beach. This tri-level galleria was originally designed by renowned architect Frank Gehry.

▲ The Arcadia Hotel, established in 1887, quickly became one of the most prestigious resorts of its day. It was named for Arcadia Bandini de Baker, the wife of Colonel R. S. Baker, cofounder of Santa Monica. The back of the hotel was designed with observatory verandas for relaxing, and each room was furnished with full bathrooms, hot and cold water, and gas and electric lighting. This four-story seaside resort was touted as having the most modern conveniences available at the time.

▲ The Arcadia Hotel gave way to several small apartment complexes and Loews Santa Monica Beach Hotel. Much like the Arcadia in its day, guests can enjoy great conveniences like the upscale fitness facility.

▲ One of the most popular spots for pleasure seekers in the city, Will Rogers State Beach once hosted one of Santa Monica's forgotten piers—the Crystal Pier, which was also alternately known as the Bristol Pier and the Hollister Pier.

▲ Though the old pier is gone, the beach is still first on most lists of favorite spots. This is a great place to try Boogie boarding or body surfing. After a day of sun and fun, it's an easy migration to one of several nearby eateries or the Third Street Promenade.

▲ This home was built in 1863 by Don Pedro Alcantara Sepulveda. The Sepulveda family was granted rights of possession to land that included all of Santa Monica. The family's lands extended from Santa Monica Canyon to today's Pico Boulevard and inland to the portion of the rolling Santa Monica mountain range that borders the San Fernando Valley.

▲ The uncomplicated, preindustrial adobe has given way to West Los Angeles postmodernism. The area has recently attracted some major television and movie studios and a new media sector development with postproduction houses.

▲ The subdivision development that was named for Pacific Electric Railway baron Henry E. Huntington started here, with workers building its streets and curbs. The area was developed by the Santa Monica Land and Electric Company. The original homes ranged in price from $16,000 to $30,000.

▲ Today, prices for homes in the Huntington Palisades neighborhood start at around $1 million. This well-established neighborhood is family oriented, and many of the traditional ranch-style homes are within walking distance of parks and the village.

▲ Visible in the background is one of many turn-of-the-century beachfront bathhouses built as private playgrounds for the throngs of bathers flocking to the cold waters of the sparkling Pacific Coast.

▲ The property upon which the majestic bathhouses of the 1920s and 1930s once sat now plays host to acres of parking lots—a testament to the sheer number of people who visit these beaches every year. Annually, a circus comes to town to entertain the locals and tourists. They set their tents up in the parking lots and attract people from the beach as well as the city.

▲ The Elks building at the corner of Main and Marine had a ballroom that could accommodate almost 2,000 people. There were apartments above and Santa Monica's first subterranean parking structure below.

▲ Today the building houses a number of popular businesses and has since been fully converted to apartments. Main Street has an eclectic collection of cafés, antiques stores, art galleries, and unique boutiques surrounded by 1920s-era Americana and twenty-first-century design. The Farmers' Market operates Sundays behind Main Street, between Hill Street and Ocean Park Boulevard. Here kids and families can enjoy eating fresh crepes while listening to live music. While the Promenade attracts more tourists, Main Street is where the locals hang out.

▲ This portrait, which originally appeared in the now-defunct *Los Angeles Herald Examiner,* was intended to showcase the grand style of living adopted by the wealthy residents of Santa Monica—in this case, the McCormicks' recently completed Gold Coast estate.

▲ Long since razed, the McCormick estate was replaced by the luxury condominiums of Ocean Drive. This area still caters to the wealthy, who see Palisades Bluffs as a peaceful, private get-away outside of the city.

▲ These are prime examples of California Spanish style, the most popular of architectural styles employed in Santa Monica residential development of the 1920s and the 1930s.

▲ Santa Monica has emerged in the last two decades as a mecca for postmodern architectural design. These staid boxes are fairly tame compared with some of the cutting-edge designs of Frank Gehry, Steven Ehrlich, and Pugh Scarpa Kodama seen throughout the city.

As the Bay Cities Guaranty Building towered above the city's busy streets, the Santa Monica Municipal Bus Lines began in 1928 and charged passengers a nickel for a ride. The bus company changed its name to Santa Monica's Big Blue Bus in 1999.

The Bay Cities Guaranty Building still stands watch over the teeming downtown streets while its clock beautifully marks the passing time under its ever-gleaming white façade. Bus service from downtown Santa Monica—now as then—provides direct access to Los Angeles attractions.

▲ The Jonathan Club was one of many private clubs that once lined this beach. Named after Jonathan Trumbull, confidant and advisor to George Washington, the Jonathan Club opened its doors in 1894.

▲ Still a privately owned structure, the building stands as a monument to the bygone glamour of Santa Monica's private clubs. Today, the club's 3,400 members can enjoy the Jonathan Beach Club and the Jonathan Town Club, which were designed by New York architects Schultze and Weaver and built in 1925.

▲ Once called "The Sunset Trail," this dusty, rambling road was one of the only ways to get from the Palisades bluffs to the beach below, and was often traversed on the back of a mule.

▲ Still serving as a vital artery, the Incline is one of Santa Monica's busiest thoroughfares, linking the Pacific Coast Highway with Ocean Avenue. The Pacific Coast Highway is a popular scenic route, with famous landmarks along the way, such as Hearst Castle, built by architect Julia Morgan in 1922 for William Randolph Hearst.

▲ In 1900, after much debate, Santa Monica citizens voted to spend $37,161 to construct the city's first headquarters for a municipal government. It was originally located at the corner of Fourth Street and Oregon Avenue (today's Santa Monica Boulevard).

▲ Built in 1938 as part of the Depression-era Works Progress Administration, the relocated City Hall is still the hub of key government officials, programs, departments, agendas, services, elections, and more. It was designed by architects Donald B. Parkinson and Joseph M. Estep. The firm of Parkinson and Parkinson is best known for its Los Angeles Art Deco masterpieces Bullocks-Wilshire and Union Station.

▲ This neighborhood was one of many post-war residential developments that provided housing for the families employed by the area's rapidly growing aerospace industry.

▲ Prices for homes on the market in this area today sell for more than a cool $2 million. Still having picket-fence charm, the lots border the first residential plots sold in the original Santa Monica property boom of 1887.

▲ This is the Breakers Beach Club just after completion in 1926. In 1934, it was reopened as the Grand Hotel—and, true to its name, it attracted celebrities of the day like Jean Harlow and Joan Crawford. It was converted to condominiums in the 1960s.

▲ The Sea Castle Apartments sit on one of the more desirable spots on the strand, just steps from the beach, in the shadow of the pier. This luxury-style building has 178 units and gives bird's-eye views of the activities on the pier and on the ocean.

Sept.17.1925

▲ Known as the Grand Dame of Santa Monica, the Casa del Mar was, by far, the most popular of the famous beach clubs of the early twentieth century. By the time this photograph was taken, Casa del Mar's membership had reached nearly two thousand and included many of the famous faces of the day.

▲ Now a luxury hotel, aside from a nip and a tuck here and there, the building hasn't strayed far from its hedonistic roots. This seven-story Renaissance-style structure has an interior that is both historical and contemporary. Elegant handmade rugs cover the floors, damask and velvet draperies adorn the windows, and wicker and rattan furnishings complete the rooms in true Roaring Twenties style.

▲ Santa Monica's Gold Coast beach clubs helped turn the sleepy, provincial town into a world-renowned leisure destination of the early to mid-twentieth century. Glassed-in private beaches, thousand-person dining rooms, and beachside service were among the amenities offered to those who could afford the membership fees.

One of the most popular destinations in the world, the Gold Coast beaches play host to tens of millions every year. Visitors enjoy the adjacent Santa Monica Pier, Muscle Beach, and a children's playground. A highlight of the area is Chess Park, where people can enjoy playing a game of chess on a life-size sidewalk game board with chess pieces that are two feet tall.

▲ Visible in the background is the Bay Cities Guaranty Building, easily identified by its famous clock tower. It opened for business in 1929 and was hailed as Santa Monica's first skyscraper.

▲ The Bay Cities Guaranty Building is still a downtown landmark. Also known as the Clock Tower, the Art Deco–style building features a zigzag pattern which follows the cornice with retracted chevron patterns and upper-story spandrels. The double-hung windows have alternating wide and narrow full façade-height pylons on both sides.

▲ The Central Tower Building, completed in 1929, was built on Fourth Avenue, on the site of the former home of Santa Monica pioneer Williamson D. Vawter. Vawter is credited with developing Santa Monica's first public transit system in the late 1800s.

▲ Fourth Street today is home to the new Transit Mall, which has energized the downtown area and made getting around a lot easier. The labyrinthine structure in the foreground is one of many public parking structures built to accommodate the crowds that also go to the adjacent Third Street Promenade, the Santa Monica Pier, and area restaurants.

▲ Before moving south to Venice Beach, the hangout for beach babes and Bobs, Muscle Beach, was originally located in the shadow of Santa Monica Pier. The move signalled a shift in popularity of beach hedonism from aerobatics to body building.

▲ Though the muscled men and women have since moved south to Venice Beach, their well-tanned legacy remains. This area is a popular spot for roller blading, and roller hockey leagues can be seen battling in the nearby parking lots.

▲ Santa Monica was founded on the legacy of its intersections. When property was being doled out, business owners laid claim to corners like this one at Santa Monica Boulevard and 3rd Street, financing and building the large commercial structures still in place today.

▲ Still important to merchants today, Santa Monica Boulevard and 3rd Street is now home to The Gap, and this location is just one of more than 4,250 of the company's stores and sees thousands of visitors per day.

▲ Built in the Queen Anne style, these stately homes were among the first to be built in the city.

▲ In cities that have grown as quickly as Santa Monica, it is inevitable that commerce often squeezes out residences. Gone are the Queen Anne homes, and the area now houses the Santa Monica Post Office, restaurants, art galleries, spas, and The Dance Doctor—a well-known studio where people can still learn to salsa.

▲ The Nebeker residence was moved from its original location here at San Vicente and Ocean in the very early years of the twentieth century. It stood as an early example of the West Coast Baroque style scattered about the city.

▲ The original Nebeker residences, moved to this block some 50 years ago, are now long gone. However, several other landmark homes are still standing, such as the Carillo House, which was built in 1925, and the MacBennel House, which was established in 1921.

▲ The building from which this photo overlooking Main Street was taken was originally commissioned by the Santa Monica Elks Lodge in 1926 as a meeting hall and clubhouse. The letters "B.P.O.E." (still inscribed in the foundation of the building) stand for Benevolent and Protective Order of Elks, one of the oldest and largest fraternal organizations in the country.

▲ Main Street has grown into one of the major links between downtown Santa Monica and Ocean Park. Since the 1920s, it has been filled with a mix of one-of-a-kind antiques shops and well-respected art galleries. The Eames Office Gallery is a local favorite; it displays the work of Charles and Ray Eames and hosts exhibitions and events throughout the world.

▲ This structure was once home to La Monica Motors, Santa Monica's sole purveyor of Rickenbacker Automobiles—a now-defunct American auto manufacturer.

▲ The site is now home to the Crocodile Café, a local hot spot.

▲ Ocean Avenue was the illustrious site of the first land auctions in the city held by Santa Monica founder Senator John P. Jones on July 10, 1875. Lots along Ocean Avenue were sold for $500 a piece, and over $80,000 worth of property was sold in the first two days.

Now one of Santa Monica's most important routes, Ocean Avenue is home to luxury hotels and condominiums, scores of restaurants, and, some would say most importantly, the entrance to the Santa Monica Pier.

▲ Located on Ocean Avenue, just across the street from the Pacific Electric Railway Depot, the Santa Monica Hotel was the city's first hotel. It burned to the ground on January 15, 1889.

▲ Though the Pacific Electric Railway Depot is gone, the spot is still a popular place to people watch. The Italian restaurant Il Fornaio now sits on the corner and has patio seating for those who want to enjoy the cool ocean breezes.

▲ The beach culture of Santa Monica has been a key feature in the life of the city. Santa Monica is credited with having the first two-man beach volleyball game. The area just north of Santa Monica Canyon has always been a haven for volleyball players, as this photo from 1924 indicates.

▲ The styles may have changed, but since Will Rogers State Beach was widened in the 1950s by the Army Corps of Engineers, it sports huge parking lots, concession stands, the famous Santa Monica bike path, and, yes, still the usual volleyball game.

▲ As the American economy began to emerge from the Great Depression, so too did the demand for affordable single-family homes. This area is a prime example of typical tract development of the time.

▲ This area, on the eastern edge of Santa Monica, is at the far end of Ocean Park, an area known collectively as "Sunset Park." Tree-lined streets and gentle hills are the setting for many single-family homes in this area.

▲ Once called Linda Vista Park, in the late 1800s the Palisades bluffs were converted into a perfect spot from which to get a bird's-eye view of the coastline. During the Spanish American War, the city's civil engineers installed large water pipes on the cliffside to give the appearance of heavy fortification in the event of an attack by Spanish warships on Santa Monica Bay.

▲ The park was originally designed to resemble a formal European garden, which included walkways, fountains, and the construction of a brick wall running the entire length of Ocean Avenue designed to block traffic from the garden's interior. The plan caused such a stir among citizens it was quickly abandoned. Instead, people can enjoy hiking, walking, inline skating, biking, and dining.

▲ One of the less conventional homes of the day, the Piano residence was modeled vaguely after early Turkish architecture.

▲ The intriguing home has since been razed and replaced by Ocean Towers. These towers, built in 1979, boast city views from the backside and ocean views from the front.

▲ With the construction of the landmark Arcadia Hotel, the promenade between Pico and Seaside Terrace became a place to be seen. In the early twentieth century, a trolley ran along this route.

▲ Waterfront apartment buildings on the right and the Pacific Ocean on the left flank this area. Bike riders, rollerbladers, skateboarders, and scooter lovers can enjoy the South Bay Bicycle Trail that extends for more than 20 miles along the coast.

SANTA MONICA PLEASURE PIER.

▲ **This is by far the most famous of all Santa Monica landmarks. The original Santa Monica Pier is the oldest and longest wood piling pier in the state. A crowd of over five thousand gathered for the Pier's dedication on September 9, 1909.**

▲ Today's Pier is actually the combination of two piers: The former Newcomb Pier built in 1916 is the section of today's Pier that holds the Carousel building—the two were attached around 1912. Having been granted status as a protected historical monument in 1973, the Pier cannot be altered or removed unless voted upon by Santa Monica citizens. Visitors can also enjoy seeing the UCLA Discovery Center Aquarium, the Pacific Park amusement park, or taking a salsa dance lesson. Over 10,000 people flock to the Pier every year for its "Twilight Dance Series" concerts.

▲ One of the city's first home-grown banking institutions, the Home Savings building was one of more than 60 bank buildings designed and decorated by renowned California architect Millard Sheets.

▲ In recent years, the Home Savings building was denied landmark status. It houses retail clothing and home furnishings stores and is part of the Third Street Promenade.

▲ Originally built for William Randolph Hearst's mistress Marion Davies in 1929, this estate was the largest on the beach. It boasted three guesthouses, two swimming pools, dog kennels, and garages big enough for a party full of people. The main house was demolished in 1957 and turned into a beach club.

▲ **Still in use today, the former Davies estate remains a tribute to a bygone era of excess and glamour. The remodeling of the estate into a community recreation and resource center has recently been delayed due to the city's low revenues.**

SANTA MONICA YACHT HARBOR

▲ **Despite the Great Depression, in 1931 Santa Monica citizens voted to approve a $690,000 bond issue to build the breakwater and yacht harbor. It was completed in 1934.**

▲ Barely visible in the center of the photo is what remains of the Breakwater; it was damaged in the severe winter storms of 1983. There are plans to replace the barrier, but construction has yet to commence.

12. TOPANGA CANYON, CAL.

Topanga Canyon has long been a haven within a haven, playing host to those wishing to live off the beaten track while still living in close proximity to the city. Adventurous souls began camping the canyons as early as 1870.

Though limited commercial and residential growth has crept slowly into the modern Canyon, local residents have managed to keep serious development at bay. Topanga Canyon has the Topanga State Park to the west, where hikers, bikers, and horseback riders can see stunning panoramic views. The park has 36 miles of trails and sites for camping, as well as picnic areas and nature trails.

▲ **McClure was originally built as a railroad tunnel connecting Olympic Boulevard and what was then called the Roosevelt Highway (today's Pacific Coast Highway).**